Machines at work

Dumper trucks

Axis education

Acknowledgements

Photographs: pages 3, 5, and 9 © Komatsu; page 9 © Trucker Jerry; page 11 © Scania; page 13 © Richard Wall; page 14 © Jason Carter; page 16 © Crown Copyright; cover and pages 18, 21, 23, 29, 30, © Volvo; page 24 © Dru Bloomfield; page 25 © Noel Jones; page 26 © MarkCanada; page 27 © Neil and Kathy Carey; page 31 © Mark Jacobsen; page 32 © cn4steel; page 33 © Codelco; page 35 © Gentech Sensors; page 35 © Fieldsports TV; page 37 © Andrew Burrows; page 39 © Chris GiantExcavator.

Every effort has been made to contact copyright holders of material reproduced in this book. Any omissions will be rectified in subsequent printings if notice is given to the publishers.

Copyright © Axis Education Ltd 2012

All rights reserved; no part of this publication may be reproduced, stored in a retrieval system, transmitted in any form, or by any means, electronic, mechanical, photocopying, recording or otherwise, without the prior permission of the publisher.

First published in Great Britain by Axis Education Ltd.

ISBN 978-1-84618-299-0

Axis Education
PO Box 459
Shrewsbury
SY4 4WZ

Email: enquiries@axiseducation.co.uk

www.axiseducation.co.uk

Dumper trucks

Dumper trucks are vehicles for carrying heavy goods such as sand, soil and stones. They are often seen on construction sites, but have many other uses including mining and military.

An off-road dumper truck.

Machines at work

There are different types of dumper truck, but what they all have in common is a tipping skip so that goods can be easily unloaded.

Some trucks tip at the front, others tip at the side. Some are rigid, others are articulated. An articulated truck has two sections connected with a flexible joint that allows the machine to turn more sharply.

Dumper trucks vary in size and capacity from mini trucks for very small loads to mega trucks that can carry tonnes of goods.

Dumper trucks

A rigid dumper truck.

An articulated dumper truck.

Machines at work

Look at any building site and you are sure to see a dumper truck. They'll be used to shift large amounts of soil, sand, stone and aggregates. In the UK, vehicles used on building sites are known as plant. Those who drive them are called plant operators.

When roads are being built or resurfaced there is often a lot of different machinery, or plant, working on the job. One of the vehicles is sure to be a dumper truck. If you ever see a mining operation, you might catch a glimpse of a monster dumper truck.

In road building it's the dumper truck that carries away the waste soil and then delivers the crushed stones called hardcore that will make a firm base for the road.

In short, if there is a need to move large amounts of soil, you are likely to see a dumper truck in action.

Dumper trucks

Hauling rubble.

The tipping skip moves for easy unloading of the dumper truck. All dumper trucks, no matter how large or how small, work in the same way.

The oldest dumper trucks were two-wheel drive with the steering wheel turning the back wheels. They were able to haul about a tonne of material and had to use gravity to tip the skip by releasing a catch next to the foot pedals.

Modern dumper trucks are easier to tip and to steer. They can carry loads as large as 10 tonnes. The arm that lifts the skip is called a ram. Some rams are telescopic to give a greater range of movement for more precise dumping.

Dumper trucks

The telescopic arm on this truck allows the driver to tip the load exactly where it needs to go on this landfill site.

In the UK road lorries that can unload using an arm or ram, are known as tipper trucks. Some tipper trucks unload backwards. Others have a mechanism that unloads sideways. Whichever direction the tipper unloads, the ram that moves the truck bed works using a hydraulic system.

The word hydraulic refers to objects that are moved or powered by a liquid – such as water or oil. The liquid pushes pistons which move the tipper arm in a dumper truck.

Dumper trucks

This truck is designed to tip its load sideways.

This truck is tipping its load backwards.

Machines at work

Some dumper trucks are built for off-road work. They can be massive vehicles, some are even bigger than a house! They are mainly used in mining. The biggest dumper trucks are too heavy to drive on roads. They are delivered to the mine in pieces and put together on site.

Dumper trucks that haul heavy loads need to be powerful. Most car engines have four or six cylinders and make less than 200 horsepower. The biggest dumper trucks can have twenty cylinders or more and can make more than 3,500 horsepower.

Dumper trucks

This truck is massive.

Dumper trucks work with other machines.

Machines at work

This man is just over 6 feet tall – these tyres are almost twice his height.

Dumper trucks

The cost of fuel must be a concern for giant dumper truck operators. An average car takes about 75 litres of fuel compared to the 3,585 litres that a giant dumper truck can hold.

Just one tyre on a giant dumper truck weighs more than a normal car and is about twice the height of an adult. You can't just open the door and drive either. Drivers of giant dumper trucks work on a machine that is taller than a normal house. They have to climb a set of steep ladders to reach the cab.

Machines at work

This truck is delivering materials for the Royal Engineers to make a road in Helmand, Afghanistan.

Dumper trucks

The British Army use a wide range of vehicles including dumper trucks. The Army categorise vehicles. 'A vehicles' are machines built for combat. 'B vehicles' aren't designed for combat and are known as the Green Fleet. 'C vehicles' are used for engineering works and include cranes, dumpers, bulldozers and tractors. Dumper trucks are C vehicles and are used in lots of ways. The army has over 60 medium dumper trucks, over 70 self-loading dumper trucks and a small fleet of mini dumpers.

The Royal Engineers use the Volvo FL12 Self Loading Dumper Truck to carry construction material and general cargo. It's a 6x6 wheeled vehicle powered by a 6 cylinder, liquid cooled, 340hp turbo diesel engine.

Machines at work

Once you've climbed on board, driving the truck is similar to driving a car.

Dumper trucks

If you can drive a manual car, driving a dumper truck will feel familiar. However, there have been accidents with dumper trucks on building sites and on roads, so safety is very important. Before driving off, you should set the seat so that you can easily reach all the gears and pedals. Make sure you have a full view of the back of the truck bed by arranging the mirrors.

Make sure the bed of the truck is completely lowered before driving off. To avoid anything falling off the back and causing an accident the load should be covered when you drive on roads. Don't drive too fast as dumper trucks can tip over on bends.

Machines at work

Once you've got going, move out of first gear as soon as possible. You'll need third gear when you get to about 10 or 15mph. Unless you're driving on a road at more than 35mph, you won't need to move up to fourth gear.

Tipping the load from a dumper truck is pretty simple. Park the truck on the level or on a slight hill with the front of the truck pointed upwards. Get out of the truck and unhook the tailgate. Go back to the cab. Next to the gear knob is a hand lever that releases the truck bed. Press the button to start the hydraulic motion that will lift the truck bed and empty the load. If the load gets stuck in the tailgate put the truck into low gear and move it forward very slowly.

Dumper trucks

Park on level ground or an upward slope before you release the load.

Machines at work

The comfort of the cab will vary from truck to truck. Modern trucks tend to be more comfortable. Volvo pride themselves on their Volvo Care Cab. They say that it is the quietest, cleanest and roomiest cab ever. The cab has great visibility due to the large rear-view mirrors. It's easy for the driver to access because it has easy-to-grip, grab handles and the cab can be easily opened from the inside. The seat can be adjusted to get the perfect fit for the driver.

With the wide angle mirrors the driver has no blind spots and can see the payload while dumping. There is even an electronic monitoring system that allows the driver to view the status of temperature, pressure levels, fuel levels and fault feedback.

Dumper trucks

You couldn't help but feel safe, comfortable and in control operating a dumper truck from this cab!

Machines at work

When roads are being built or repaired there will always be a dumper truck on site. Once bulldozers have moved the rubble and scrapers have flattened the ground it's the dumper truck that moves in to take the waste away.

Here the old tarmac is being fed directly into the truck bed.

Dumper trucks

After the waste has gone the dumper trucks come back to deliver the hardcore that will make a firm base for the road.

An articulated Astra dumper truck.

Machines at work

Colin drives a dumper truck at an iron ore mine in Australia. It's hot and dusty outside, so the air-conditioned cab is ideal. He works with other plant drivers. The digger operator loads up the trucks.

These machines may look small in this picture, but each dumper truck is taller than an average house.

Colin transports both iron ore and waste products from the mine to a nearby unit where the ore is processed. The mine has lots of giant dumper trucks including the Caterpillar 797 and the Komatsu 930E. It's a big operation, but it is also a long way from any big towns or cities. Colin works a twelve-hour shift. The company he works for gives drivers long holidays to make up for these hard shifts.

Colin ready for his shift.

Machines at work

You don't have to have any particular qualifications to become a dumper truck driver. Some companies like you to have some GCSEs (maths, English and technology will be the most helpful). Most people join a construction company as an apprentice so they get to earn money while they learn the job. Once you've mastered driving a dumper truck, you are likely to be trained to operate other plant such as bulldozers and diggers.

Wage rates are agreed each year. The basic pay is good and you can sometimes earn more by doing overtime. With bigger companies there is the chance to become a supervisor. Some plant operators go on to set up their own business. If you are prepared to travel, there are job opportunities overseas too.

The days can be long and you are likely to work far away from towns and cities, so you need to remember to take drinks and lunch with you.

Dumper trucks

Having a well-earned break.

Machines at work

At the start of every shift the driver is told what he or she will be doing by a supervisor. If the job is complex there may be a written plan that the operators must follow. This driver is going to be moving earth for a new housing estate.

Checking the plan.

The largest dumper truck in the world is the Caterpillar 797F. It has a load capacity of 363 tonnes and drives at a top speed of 42mph. It is mainly used by companies mining coal, copper, iron and gold.

The Caterpillar 797F is huge.

The machine is moved to the site in pieces. It takes six or seven articulated lorries to move the engine, frame, axles and differential. The cab goes on one lorry but the six tyres require two lorries, and the dumper body requires four lorry loads. In total, one 797 needs 12-13 lorry loads to move it to the customer site.

Caterpillar send a team of mechanics to the site to put the 797 together. The dumper body is welded together – that takes seven to ten days. It takes another 20 days for a team of seven mechanics working in three shifts around the clock, seven days per week to assemble the truck. If a 797 has to be moved from one job site to another, it has to be taken apart and put back together again as it's too heavy to drive on public roads.

Transporting the hull takes a massive low loader.

Dumper trucks

The price of each 797 varies but is in the range of £2.5–4 million. The machine needs tyres, each costing about £26,500. A puncture would be expensive!

An expensive fleet!

Machines at work

There are mini dumper trucks too. The JCB Groundhog is a utility vehicle. It's a 6x4 with a top speed of 18mph and is used in many industries.

The turf-tyred version is used by football clubs to transport cones, footballs and poles during daily training sessions as well as for moving other supplies. It's ideal for moving people and loads across delicate ground. This version is also popular at golf clubs.

Gamekeepers prefer rough terrain tyres as they need to go off-road to do feed rounds and check traps. They may also use a truck for transport on shoot days.

No matter what type of grounds care, a utility vehicle is ideal if you need to move people, equipment and materials over ground you don't want to damage. It can also be used in farming. On big construction sites it's perfect for moving people quickly to where they need to be.

Dumper trucks

Ideal for forestry.

Perfect for feed rounds in gamekeeping.

Machines at work

If you're never going to have a career as a dumper truck driver, you can still find out what one is like to drive by going to a special theme park. Diggerland has four sites in the UK in Kent, Devon, Durham and Yorkshire where you can ride and drive full size construction machinery. You'll be guided by trained staff. You don't even need a driving licence to take part!

If you're over 17 and feeling brave, you can enter dumper truck racing events. Each competitor takes part in at least 2 race heats against the clock and the other competitors. The fastest times will qualify to reach a grand final.

It's all a lot of fun and will give you a taster of what it would feel like to work as a dumper truck driver.

Dumper trucks

You have to drive through the obstacles.

As it gets dark you need to switch on the lights.

Technical specification – Komatsu 930E

The Komatsu 930E is the best selling ultra class (giant) dumper truck in the world.

Power	2,701 horsepower
Engine	16-cylinder turbo-diesel
Top speed	40mph (64kph)
Payload	290,000kg
Fuel tank capacity	4,500 litres
Price	£3,250,000
Weight when empty	9,608kg
Operating weight	504,394kg
Tyres	53/80 R63
Tyre weight	26,127kg

Dumper trucks

The Komatsu 930E.

Glossary

aggregates	a term used for sand, gravel and crushed stone that are used in construction
apprentice	someone who has agreed to work for a skilled person for a particular period of time and often for low payment, in order to learn that person's skills
assemble	to put together
gamekeeper	a person whose job is to take care of wild animals and birds that are kept especially for hunting
hardcore	stone that is compacted and used as a base in road building
horsepower/hp	a unit for measuring the power of an engine
overtime	time that you spend working in your job in addition to your normal working hours
payload	the carrying capacity of a vehicle
plant	a term used for machinery and equipment used in a workplace, especially in construction
plant operator	someone whose job it is to drive machinery such as dumper trucks, bulldozers, loaders and so on
supervisor	someone who is in charge of others to make sure work is being carried out correctly
telescopic	made of parts that slide over each other so that the whole thing can be made longer or shorter